THE INNER COMPASS

14 Leadership Secrets to Finding Your True North

I0471026

THE INNER COMPASS

14 Leadership Secrets to Finding Your True North

DIANE KUCALA

18 17 16 15 14 13   10 9 8 7 6 5 4 3 2 1

The Inner Compass: 14 Leadership Secrets to Finding Your True North

ISBN: 978-1492926733
Copyright ©2013 by Diane Kucala

Published by TJ Associates, LLC
PO Box 131172, Carlsbad CA 92013

www.blueprintleadership.com

Printed in the United States of America. All rights reserved under International Copyright Law. Contents and/or cover may not be reproduced in whole or in part in any form without the express written consent of the Publisher.

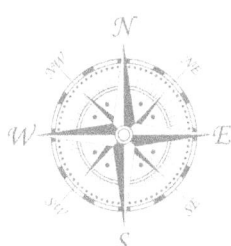

Contents

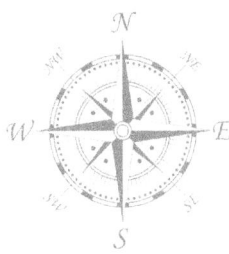

Humility:
An Essential Strength

> Humility: To Appreciate the Strengths
> and Competencies of Others

"Oh, he's so humble! I just love doing business with people like him."

If you're like most people, that statement doesn't sound accurate because, for whatever reason, humility is not an attitude that we typically associate with business success. We perceive a humble person as soft, a pushover, or weak-willed, whereas we perceive successful businesspeople as aggressive, strong, go-getters.

This is a misperception of humility. Nothing could be further from the truth.

The best way I have heard humility defined is, **"Humility is not thinking less of yourself, but thinking of yourself less."**[1] In other words, humility does nothing to dull the edge of our abilities or our drive. Instead it refocuses them on something that is truly more fulfilling. It aims them at a greater cause, one that benefits more than just ourselves, bringing benefit to our workforce, partners, customers, and—yes—ourselves.

Humility frees us from one of the most limiting factors commonly found in leaders today: Ego. Consider the following contrasts:

Ego:

- Ego operates out of pride and arrogance, injuring the people around them in pursuit for the top.

- Ego seeks to elevate oneself. This impedes service to the greater cause.

- Ego feels the need to do things "my way." This need slows the speed of the journey as people wrestle over methodology and hold tight reins on process steps.

- Ego motivates the promotion of one's own name and accomplishments. This puts self at the center of conversation and interactions.

Humility:

- Humility operates out of the motivation to make a difference in the world and in the people encountered. Humility seeks to remove obstacles, instead of being one.

- Humility sets its sights on the fulfillment of noble, big-picture goals, independent of personal recognition gained along the way.

- Humility relinquishes concern over methodology to focus on removal of obstacles. The front position carries the responsibility to clear the path for successful outcomes.

- Humility embraces the best contributions of everyone on the team regardless of title, position, or expertise, giving credit where credit is due. It flows from a security that enjoys celebrating the contributions of others.

Given the option, who wouldn't rather work with a humble person than an egotistical one? Yet, humility is more than an altruistic attitude to take in business. That is, it isn't *just* the right thing to do—it also generates better results.

Results can be like those of John Wooden, who is known perhaps as much for his leadership as he is for his success as a basketball coach. His success as a coach included ten NCAA national championships (seven in a row from 1967-73), a record 88 consecutive victories spanning three seasons, only one losing season in forty years of coaching, and many more records and achievements that may never be broken or repeated.[2]

His success is always tied to his leadership ability, filling eight books (including a children's book), but summed up by his Pyramid of Success. This pyramid is made up of 15 personal qualities that he believed brought success. One third of them—friendship, loyalty, cooperation, and team spirit—required his athletes to choose humility and put team above self.[3] His humble leadership through these principles was so significant that he was even awarded the Presidential Medal of Freedom, the highest civilian honor in America.[4]

A humble attitude drives cohesion and collaboration in all teams. Jim Collins studied 1,435 Fortune 500 companies and identified 11 as superior organizations (see *Good to Great: Why Some Companies Make the Leap and Others Don't*[5]). The Magellan group[6] followed up the Collins study by studying 11 self-identified Servant Leadership companies. All 22 companies had one thing in common: they exhibited incredible leadership skills founded upon an attitude of humility. Both studies conclude that **the most effective leaders carry an amazing ability to both radiate deep personal humility and carry an intense personal will to leave a mark on their community**.

What this tells us is that, while ego can look good at first glance, it cannot accomplish anything deeper or more meaningful than that, falling short of those things that truly set companies apart as leaders and contributors. **Only humility has this kind of power.** Yes, I said that humility is powerful, certainly more powerful than ego.

An exponential multiplication of creativity and productivity is awaiting us. All it requires is that we leave ego behind and embrace humility.

John Wooden

 Ask college basketball's greatest coaches who is the best coach of all time. They will all agree, the answer is John Wooden. That has to be the answer. After all, he won ten championships. If you take the four coaches with the next most championships and add them together you only get 13; none of them even reached halfway to Wooden's mark. What's more, Wooden won his ten championships in a twelve-year span, and he won them with every kind of team and style of play imaginable.[7]

Those facts are significant all by themselves when we consider Wooden. But they're most revealing as perspective when we consider one of his most profound characteristics: his humility. One journalist powerfully saw this firsthand, as recorded in the following account:

Coach Wooden's wife Nell was terminally ill and had come to the Final Four knowing it was likely going to be her last one. She was in a wheelchair, and all weekend, Coach Wooden pushed her around trying to see as many friends as possible.

Late one night in the coaches' hotel, the Woodens said their goodnights to a group of friends. The place was packed even though it was well after midnight. Seeing Coach Wooden pushing his wife in the direction of the elevators, someone started to clap. By the time the Woodens had reached the elevators, everyone was clapping.

Coach Wooden stopped and turned Nell so she could face everyone. The two of them waved their hands and nodded their thanks.

Years later, I asked Coach Wooden if he remembered that moment, and for an instant, I thought he had forgotten because he was silent. Finally he said: "Oh yes, I remember it. That was a very sad time for me, but having all those people do that so spontaneously, well, it meant a lot to me and to Nell. There is nothing quite like the respect of your peers."[8]

Such was Wooden's humility. While others knew him as a legend, he recognized them as peers, a status they would never claim for themselves, but which he granted freely.

What do You Think?

1. Why is humility powerful?

2. When is it hardest to be humble?

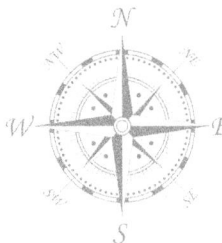

Respect:
Where Personhood and Production Meet

> *Respect: To Value and Show Regard
> Toward Others*

What goes around comes around; we all know that. But this is most evident when it comes to respect.

It's a simple fact: Respect breeds respect. If you show respect for someone, they will most often return the favor. This is one reason respect is such a powerful value for leaders to cultivate in the workplace.

It is true that it's easier to respect others when they have shown respect to us, but that works both ways. We are easier to respect once we have demonstrated respect toward others. Albert Einstein said, "I speak to everyone in the same way, whether he is the garbage man or the president of the university."[5] **What makes us great leaders is that we show respect first.** Do not be a leader because of your authority alone; instead be a leader by your character, action and example.

To do this, we need to ask what respect is and how we recognize it. Respect is essentially the recognition of another's value, which means that it can be demonstrated in two significant ways.

First, we can respect someone for their inherent worth according to their core identity, considered completely apart from what they do. We see from Einstein's words that he clearly recognized that each person has the same value regardless of their role in life, and he did this despite his extensive list of lauded accomplishments. Dr. Seuss also expressed this well in his children's book, *Horton Hears a Who!*, saying, "A person's a person, no matter how small."[1]

In the marketplace, **we miss the mark if we assign respect based only upon status, intellect, achievement, or contribution**. These are worthy performance standards, and they are worthy of respect, but they are not the gateway for respect.

This is important because when we grant respect based only on what people do without consideration for the inherent worth of people, we create an environment that celebrates performance but undervalues people. This kind of environment chokes the lifeblood out of compassion, empathy, and care for people. It destroys authenticity and trust. If we are to create and keep the kind of leaders who establish long-term organizational success, we esteem value correctly—recognizing inner worth (who a person is) before we evaluate and celebrate achievement (what a person does).

Once we establish that all people inherently have value, the next level of respect is valuing what people do. The importance of developing a foundation of respect for the worth of each individual in no way minimizes the importance of performance and achievement.

Authenticity and trust are foundational, but they are not enough by themselves. To be successful, people and organizations must energize and maximize the skills, talents, and abilities of every person on the team. The result is increased organizational power and individual sense of fulfillment.

Everyone gains when we optimize and respect what people contribute.

Building high-performance teams is about respecting people for who they are (BE) **and** what they contribute (DO). When we respect people at the BE level, we build trust. When we respect at the DO level, we leverage the strengths of each contributor, which means that everyone thrives!

Leaders are respected by their followers when the leader first demonstrates that their followers are worthy people with intrinsic value. People follow us because we care about them as unique individuals. There is incredible power in a leader who recognizes the inherent value in his followers and treats them accordingly. Leaders are also respected when they value the good ideas and amazing competencies of followers.

Soon, the followers begin to treat one another with the same respect that they have been shown. The workplace develops a culture where people appreciate what their co-workers contribute to the common goals and, because they feel accepted, needed, and appreciated, they enjoy coming to work—and work hard while they are there.

Respect also brings out the best in your employees because it recognizes what they contribute—and not just their history of contribution, but their future potential contributions. Soon, productivity increases and reputation grows. This reputation influences the client base positively and opens more doors of opportunity.

When all this happens, business is as business should be— thriving and enjoyable at the level of individual employees, and growing and profitable at the large-scale bottom line. This is the melding of the best of both worlds—personhood and production—and a key to it all is respect.

Respect: SAS

What does SAS, one of the largest privately-owned software companies in the world, name as its greatest source of success? Founder and CEO Jim Goodnight makes it clear: "Ninety-five percent of my assets drive out the gate every evening.......The creativity they bring to SAS is a competitive advantage for us."[2]

This value for the workforce has been engrained in SAS's culture from the very beginning, when Goodnight insisted that workers received individual offices, break rooms stocked with free refreshments, on-site exercise facilities and daycare centers, and a team of company physicians and nurses.[3] SAS has held and even expanded this tradition ever since while posting 37 consecutive years of record earnings.[4]

The SAS culture of respect has not been untested, however. When recession hit in 2009, businesses stopped investing in major software upgrades, and most software companies began laying off employees. Workers at SAS began to worry, so Goodnight held a company-wide webcast to pledge that there would be no layoffs in 2009, though he would need everyone's help to reduce expenses. That promise extended to include 2010 as well. When employees felt secure about their jobs again, creativity flowed and the business prospered. In fact, 2009 was one of their top three most profitable years.[5]

Business and leadership consultant Mark C. Crowley describes the SAS culture this way: "More than anything, SAS has found that by being an especially benevolent and respectful organization, they consistently produce the most optimal workplace performance. Their highly non-traditional insight is that workers instinctively and positively respond to an organization that routinely demonstrates that they matter and are individually valued."[6]

Voices within SAS agree, as stated by Jack Poll, a 28-year employee, "When people are treated as if they're important and truly make a difference, their loyalty and engagement soar."[7] This loyalty and engagement lead to low turnover rates, which leads to greater profitability, which can be invested right back into the workforce, which further entrenches loyalty and engagement.

This is how business should be, and it all begins with respect in the workforce.

What do You Think?

1. What qualities do you most respect in a person?

2. What undesirable attributes in others challenge your will to value their inner worth?

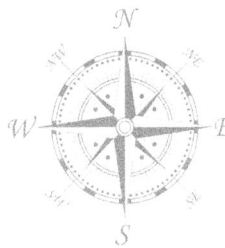

Honesty:
Powerful, Compassionate Perspective

> *Honesty: To Be Sincere and Truthful*

All of us likely remember the childhood story about the boy who cried wolf. If we have children, we've probably even repeated it to teach our own children about the importance of honesty. What many of us perhaps haven't realized yet is that the more responsibility we carry, the more important honesty becomes.

What's more, **genuine honesty is more than just simple truth**. Honesty is shaped by two extra elements—experiences and compassion. A recent experience I had with a newly acquired client illustrates this perfectly. This client just had a bad experience with another coach. The coach set up a series of four calls over a period of two months. Unfortunately, the coach missed two of the four scheduled calls due to a family member's illness. On both occasions, the coach failed to notify the client ahead of time and did not follow up in a timely manner after the missed calls. When the client expressed concern about this, the coach perceived that the client was not compassionate and had unrealistic expectations since the coach was facing hardship. The client's and the coach's perspectives of truth were so incompatible that the relationship was terminated. So, what happened?

In some cases, **truth is complex.** The coach's truth was filtered through "family emergency." The client's truth was filtered through "personal accountability." These are not incompatible truths, but because the two parties could not reconcile their perspectives, full truth eluded both of them and the relationship ended badly.

We see from this example that one aspect of truth is seeing reality with 20/20 vision, unfiltered by emotional or distorted bias, which neither the coach nor the client did in our example. However, truth is only valuable to the extent that it uplifts people to a higher level of living. The coach and client might have seen the other person's perspective on the truth of the situation, but that would never matter unless they cared enough about the other person to act based on the other's perspective instead of solely their own.

All of us know people who speak "truth," but without diplomacy. This kind of truth hits like a whip and demoralizes the spirit of another person. That truth may actually be reality, but more likely it is one's distorted view of reality. In either case, truth without compassion is just a whipping tool. It doesn't serve to uplift, grow, and develop another person's capacity. **Truth without compassion is often brutal and falls short of genuine honesty.**

Hopefully we have experienced times when someone has approached us with compassion and with our best interest in mind to share a blind spot or an area of development. As the discussion unfolds, we realize this person is standing with us out of concern, and that they believe in us enough to courageously invite us to a heightened level of character or performance. We understand that the person is really acting unselfishly for our benefit. This compassionate expression of the truth woos us to embrace the feedback.

Genuine honesty—compassionate truth driven by another's best interest—is still not always easy to accept, nor is it easy to give. **It takes real courage to give and receive genuine honesty.** Too often, people avoid the truth because they don't want to risk offending someone or they don't want to expend the energy it will take to compassionately share truth. Nevertheless, withholding truth for either of these reasons is dishonest. Sometimes honesty requires sacrifice, but the payoff is always greater than the cost.

Organizations get into trouble when people do not exhibit honesty in day-to-day operations. They break trust with their client base or with the people they serve. We have historically seen this in both government and business. Dishonesty was the reason that President Nixon had to declare, "I am not a crook," and was eventually forced to resign from office. Dishonesty was the reason that Enron collapsed. Dishonesty was a big contributor to the recent housing collapse, which in turn was the main reason for starting the second decade of the 21st century in recession. Dishonesty earned Lance Armstrong a lifetime ban from cycling and forced him to separate himself from his Livestrong organization.

Sometimes people are dishonest intentionally to be self-serving, but much more frequently, dishonesty manifests because individuals are afraid to confront the truth. They may start thinking things like, "What if I am seeing this wrong? What ramifications might this have on me and my career? I'm just part of a big, broken system that I have no control over."

We have known the effects of dishonesty from childhood, and now we see that the ramifications only increase as responsibility increases. **We must be the courageous ones who lead the way** to genuine honesty in our organizations, stepping in to make the small corrections before they become large mistakes, challenging those around us to expand perceptions of reality so that we can use truth to serve others. In so doing, we will avoid the pitfalls of dishonesty and gain the power of compassionate truth framed in a more complete perspective.

Honesty: Andrew Mason

Andrew Mason has every appearance of a serial entrepreneur, despite the fact that he graduated from Northwestern University with a degree in music and not business.[1] He founded Groupon when he was 27,[2] and it exploded to become one of the fastest growing companies in recent history. After only four and a half years of business, Groupon's forecasted revenue for 2013 is $2.55 billion.[3]

Despite this amazing growth, Groupon failed to meet shareholder expectations for several quarters in a row, and Mason was fired in early 2013. He'll tell you so himself. In fact, in a letter to his company the day it happened, he wrote, "I was fired today. If you're wondering why…the events of the last year and a half speak for themselves. As CEO, I am accountable."[4]

Mason had so many excuses he could have made for his firing. He's young. He has no formal educational background in business. It was his first successful startup business, and rapid growth is difficult to manage. But he didn't take any of these options. Instead, he embraced honesty, taking full blame for failures in his company while talking up the potential of what he left behind.

"You are doing amazing things at Groupon, and you deserve the outside world to give you a second chance. I'm getting in the way of that. A fresh CEO earns you that chance," he wrote. "For those who are concerned about me, please don't be—I love Groupon, and I'm terribly proud of what we've created. I'm OK with having failed at this part of the journey."[5]

Mason's decision to handle this difficult situation with such candid honesty makes this failure appear to be merely a lesson on the path of further success. He demonstrates what it means to embrace the brutal truth with courage and to act on that truth with compassion toward others. I suspect, we will hear lots more from Andrew Mason in the future. He is an honest leader.

What do You Think?

1. How have you benefited from compassionate truth in your life?

2. What are some inhibitors that prevent you from being more honest at work, home and in your community?

Trustworthiness:
The Foundation for Powerful Relationships

> *Trustworthiness: To Have a Reputation of Being Faithful to Another's Best Interest*

There is perhaps no soft skill that has more direct implications for the hard bottom line than the skill of building trust. Simply put, trust is the catalyst for growth of any kind, both at work and at home.

If trust is so important, why don't we hear more about it in business school and corporate staff meetings? Perhaps because it is such an intangible concept. Trust revolves around how we feel in any given situation. Yet despite it being intangible, we do measure trust. We can all identify times when trust is high and times when trust is low. As we examine those high and low moments of trust, what defines those moments more than the trust we give is our perception of how worthy another person is of being trusted.

The question is not so much whether each individual will place their trust in us; it is about **how trustworthy we are perceived to be**. Individuals trust at differing times and tempos. The truth is that while we have no control over the trust others extend toward us, we can take responsibility for how trustworthy we prove ourselves to be.

Trust is not an automatic response in every situation. It is built upon experiences that are demonstrations of two aspects of our personhood—who we *are* and what we *do*.

Important elements of **who we are** that demonstrate trustworthiness include such things as honesty, respect, integrity, humility, justice, honor, and courage. Some questions that can help us gauge the trustworthiness we communicate to others include:

- Does what I say align with truth?

- Are my actions consistent with my personal values and that of my organization?

- Do I uplift and support others?

- Am I willing to get whatever I can for others, even at my own' expense?

- Am I willing to do what is right regardless of the consequences?

Important elements of **what we do** that demonstrate trustworthiness include such things as accountability, commitment, perseverance, emotional intelligence, communication, and consistency. Some questions that can help us gauge the trustworthiness we communicate through what we do include:

- Do I take responsibility for outcomes?

- Do I do whatever it takes to meet deadlines and agreements?

- Do I maintain a safe and respectful environment when I communicate with people?

- Do I make decisions in a timely manner?

- Do I communicate feelings, project status and performance honestly?

Now, take the pressure off yourself by realizing that no one is perfectly trustworthy. We all fall short of the mark. Yet, this is a great exercise in determining where we can enhance our trustworthiness, and therefore our success.

It is important to realize that trustworthiness is not binary—it falls within a continuum. **The more experiences we accumulate of trustworthiness, the more solidly people view us as trustworthy.** The good news is that this is completely in our control in establishing trust bonds. Most people endure minor infractions (and sometimes these can even strengthen the bond, if handled properly). We need to take care, however, to avoid a major infraction that could severely break trust.

Fortunately, relationships built on accumulated experiences of trustworthiness hold resilient power. Speaking from personal experience, major infractions can be restored with time, effort, and forgiveness. **Every day and every interaction holds the potential to build trust or break trust. It all comes down to whether we will choose to take actions that prove our trustworthiness.**

This building process takes time and it takes trust. Are you taking the time to build trust?

Trustworthiness: Warren Buffet

"The chains of habit are too light to be noticed until they are too heavy to be broken," says multi-billionaire investor Warren Buffet.[1] This principle is why Buffet, the business magnate, investor and philanthropist known as the "Oracle of Omaha", values the character of an individual or business more highly than anything else. It is also the secret to his success as an investor, as he diligently forged good habits of his own and watched carefully for businesses that also operated with good habits.

These habits have worked over time to make Buffet known as a trustworthy leader. He's reliable, dependable, follows through on what he says, and lives out his stated values. Perhaps more telling, even as the stock market is known for being untrustworthy, Buffet's investments are the opposite, far outgaining the market in general over time.

Not long ago, Buffet made a decision that gives us a clear example of what it takes to develop and maintain trustworthiness as a business leader. As with us all, Buffet has a personal life, and just like the rest of us, he probably would rather keep his personal life private instead of sharing intimate details with the public.

However, because Buffet's company—Berkshire-Hathaway— is a publicly traded company, when Buffet was diagnosed with prostate cancer, he determined to share that information. He easily could have chosen to keep it confidential as many other Fortune 100 companies CEO's have done. After all, the diagnosis was that his cancer was in no way life-threatening.

Warren decided to reveal his diagnosis allowing traders to decide for themselves how to weigh any risk to their investments, showing faithfulness to their best interest above his own. This decision was just one in a long line of consistent actions—illustrating proven trustworthiness founded in a life of character.

What do You Think?

1. How do you define trustworthiness?

2. What one thing can you do to create a habit of trustworthiness?

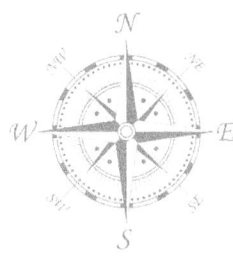

Courage:
The Guts of Leadership

> *Courage: To Remain Unmoved by Adverse Situations*

One of the most highly regarded and sought after attributes in our society is courage. Leaders, perhaps more than any other group of people, find courage to be an absolute requirement. In fact, I would go so far as to say that **if you have courage, you will find people following you**.

Many people experience fear and anxiety as a part of their daily lives. These are both very common in our personal and professional lives. We have all learned different coping mechanisms for fear and anxiety, but it all boils down to having courage—courage to keep going when you just fell flat on your face, courage to share bad news, courage to trust, and courage to take risks.

Courage can reveal itself in all sorts of different ways. To be an effective leader, we must remember that every deci sion we make impacts others, regardless of whether it is in our families, communities, churches, athletic teams, or our workplace. Decisions at work usually impact us at three levels: individually, departmentally, and organizationally.

Individually: Courageous choices become courageous habits, and vice versa. When we make a courageous choice and see the powerful reward that comes from it, it helps us to be courageous again the next time.

Departmentally: Those around you will see the tone you set for making decisions and will only rise up to your example. Any lack of courage will stifle creativity, ingenuity, and innovation in those around you, bogging your departments down in the way things have always been done.

Organizationally: Lack of courage robs your organization of achieving its fullest potential because growth requires conflict and change. When your employees see a lack of courage in you, it leaves them stagnant, disconnected from vision, and discouraged from stepping into their own potential.

Take a stand today to be courageous! You have skills and abilities. You have a responsibility to share your full potential, even if that means stepping out of your comfort zone. If you are good with kids, then serve in your community to help youngsters. If you are detail-oriented and analytical, then come alongside someone implementing an idea. If you are a good mentor coach, then reach out to people who seek development. Choose courage and take the risks to find outlets for the things at which you most naturally excel! Winston Churchill once said, "Success is not final, failure is not fatal: it is the courage to continue that counts."[1] Have courage and become what you have been designed to be.

Maya Angelou said, "Courage: the most important of all the virtues because without courage, you can't practice any other virtue consistently."[2] Without courage, we waver in the mission, we falter when the going gets rough, we listen to the dissenters when we should move forward.

The recent movie *Lincoln* reminds us of how courage partnered with vision to make Abraham Lincoln the history-shaping man we remember him to be. Time and again, he faced opposition, even from within his own party and from his closest friends. He even faced opposition from his own family. Nevertheless, because of courage, Lincoln persevered. Because of the courageous choices he made, the 1860s were marked by even greater civil rights advances than the 1960s, advances that continue to ripple through the world even today.

Lincoln took risks. The importance of the mission drew him beyond his comfort zone to do what was right despite obstacles and personal ramifications. Courage will grow in us as well when we discover a vision worth spending our lives pursuing. Our discontent at living with a vision unfulfilled will propel us with courage through difficulties until it is finally attained.

What can you do to influence a culture of courage? Now, I am not encouraging you to take uncalculated risks within your company. Instead, I am encouraging you to embrace the vision of what is possible! See what has potential beyond your current comfort zone.

People with courage are willing to "go where no one has gone before" and are not afraid to experience some setbacks to do so. If you are not the "forger of a new path" in your organization, be the person who supports courageous vision and leverage your talents alongside theirs to discover a new frontier. Courage is about believing for something beyond our comfort zone and embracing the talents of others and our own to take hold of that destiny.

Courage is a choice. The reward is greatness!

Courage: Ronnie Andrews

The pink ribbon is pervasive in our culture these days, and many people personally know what it means because they or a loved one have been affected by breast cancer. Very few, however, have been able to do something about the dreaded disease. Ronnie Andrews is such a person.

As a child, Ronnie became very close to his grandmother, or Memaw, as he called her. He was eleven when she first was diagnosed with breast cancer. When she saw how, even as a kid, he poured over research to learn more about it, she said to him, "Ronnie, you're smart enough to fix this." He promised her that when he grew up, he would do just that.

His pursuit for a cure would lead him to work as VP of Sales and Marketing for Roche Diagnostic Corporation, overseeing a national division working on the genetic mapping of HIV. He saw how this technology would have applications for cancer as well, but after four years, he felt that what he was doing had too small an impact directly on patients. When a small, nearly-bankrupt company called Chromavision contacted him to ask him to take charge, he courageously left what many would call a dream job—to pursue his real dream.

Under Andrew's guidance, the company, now re-named Clarient, grew in five years to a $100 million dollar company. Soon, GE bought the company for almost $600 million, and they now test 150,000 cancer samples every year, helping provide individualized care for cancer patients throughout the country.

Ronnie Andrews drew courage from the passion in his heart to fulfill the commitment he made to his grandmother. Though he, like Lincoln, faces tremendous adversity, he wouldn't relent on the promise, the vision. That courage now benefits millions of cancer patients and their families across the world. And, the mission continues.

What do You Think?

1. Where do you need courage to achieve an important outcome?

2. What are the fears, anxieties or hurdles that you need to overcome? Who/what can help you?

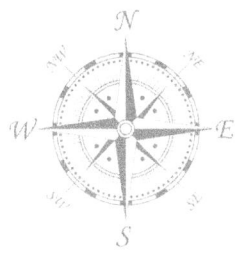

Commitment:
Holding Fast to Vision

Commitment: To Deliver on
Promises Made

We view the organization's purpose, vision, mission, strategies, and values as a promise we make to our customers and we are collectively dedicated to delivering what we have promised.

A wise man once said, "Without vision, people cast off restraint." What he was saying is that only a clear vision of our future has the power to restrain us to the path that will get us there.

When we lack this kind of vision, one of the first things to go out the window is commitment. Commitment is rarely convenient. Commitment battles with adages like, "Opportunity knocks but once," forcing us to decide whether we will deliver on promises already given or break them for what appear to be better opportunities.

But, to use another adage, appearances can be deceiving, for commitment is so powerful that the immediate payoff for broken promises rarely, if ever, outweighs the benefit of commitments fulfilled over time.

The secret is that commitment is the glue in relationship, the power that gives value to loyalty. Customers want to have a trusted and open relationship, to feel valued and esteemed. They want your full attention and concentration. Only commitment satisfies these desires.

I won't pretend that commitment is easy. It's not. In fact, commitment requires intentional choice and sacrifice, being willing to give up self-interests, comfort, and convenience for the sake of keeping our word. It requires us to take a handshake as seriously as we would a contract.

When commitment is this difficult, even painful sometimes, we need to understand more clearly the long-term benefits so we will stay true to our word even when it's hard. And, really, examples are all around us of why commitment is so important.

Consider the world of investments, where we all know that staying in for the long haul is the way to actually make money. One story to illustrate this comes from someone I know who attended college with twin brothers. These twin brothers had a grandmother who, when they were young, bought them a little bit of stock in a small company called Microsoft. By the time my acquaintance knew them in college, they were both millionaires, having earned their entire fortune through payments of commitment.

Or consider the natural world around us. Did you know that if you keep uprooting and replanting a tree, its root system becomes dwarfed and will not grow as it would if left planted in one place? This lack of root system prevents the tree from getting adequate nutrition from the soil and leaves it vulnerable to disease and wind. Only when a tree is "committed" to one spot in the ground can it flourish and become all it can possibly be.

Og Mandino, in his book, *Og Mandino's University of Success*, describes the benefits of long-term commitment. Mandino tells the story of Raphael Solano and his companions who were looking for diamonds in a Venezuela river bed. Solano claims he had picked up about 999,999 rocks and was ready give up on this pursuit—his only opportunity to bring financial benefit to his very poor family. His companions said, "Pick up one more and make it an even million." That "millionth" rock was "The Liberator," the largest and purest diamond ever found. Mandino writes, "I think he (Solano) must have known a happiness that went beyond the financial. He had set his course; the odds were against him; he had persevered; he had won. He had not only done what he had set out to do—which is a reward in itself—but he had done it in the face of failure and obscurity."[1]

Commitment has its own reward of fulfillment, bringing significance (which is more than mere achievement) and stability to a world that is paying the price of unpredictability and change for the sake of convenience. Imagine for a moment what our culture would be like if everyone held commitment in higher esteem. What would business look like if you knew you could rely on your teammates 100 percent of the time? What would government look like if you actually trusted the words of politicians? What would family look like if divorce were the rarity instead of being so common? What would the impact of this be on children a generation from now who grew up with confidence and security because everyone at home, school, and work demonstrated commitment in everything they did?

Listen, I know this sounds outlandish, but if we discount it as impossible then we certainly won't ever have this as our future. However, if we believe that this vision is possible and we simply choose to be committed, we create this future by choosing to be committed in our own lives.

We don't want to make a law out of commitment. There are times that unforeseen events happen and we have to adjust our schedules. But if we understand the future that commitment produces, it will help us make the right adjustments when necessary and hold to our commitments when adjustments are merely convenient.

Tom Landry once said, "Leadership is getting someone to do what they don't want to do, to achieve what they want to achieve.[2]

Commitment is the only way to get there! If you're looking for a practical way to cultivate commitment, consider the following progression:

> "Watch your thoughts, for they become words.
> Watch your words, for they become actions.
> Watch your actions, for they become habits.
> Watch your habits, for they become character.
> Watch your character, for it becomes your destiny."[3]

Commitment: Jim Sinegal

The CEOs of today's companies face pressure from every side. On them rests the heavy burden of satisfying employees, managers, shareholders, and customers without sacrificing the mission, vision, and values of the company. It can be all too easy to lose focus while trying to juggle so many priorities.

Jim Sinegal is an example of a successful leader who has resisted the pressure to shave his commitments. He co-founded Costco in 1983 on a model of selling a limited number of items at low cost and high volume while paying workers well, charging for membership, and targeting upscale shoppers.[4] For thirty years he has held these values in the face of great opposition from both his chief competitor—Sam's Club, owned by the retail giant Wal-Mart—and his biggest critics: Wall Street.

What decisions have come under the most intense fire? One issue is how well Costco takes care of its employees, who earn an average of seven dollars an hour more than Wal-Mart employees, and have such excellent benefits that 85 percent of employees are covered by the company's healthcare program and 91 percent are covered by retirement plans.[5] Wall Street analysts say Costco should lower employee pay in order to give more to shareholders. Sinegal disagrees. "We think when you take care of your customer and your employees, your shareholders are going to be rewarded in the long run... I care about the stock price. But we're not going to do something for the sake of one quarter that's going to destroy the fabric of our company and what we stand for," he said.[6]

Jim Sinegal held onto the Costco vision even withstanding the pressures of Wall Street. That commitment to core values is what has defined both Sinegal and his company, and it has made them the industry leader everyone wishes they could be.

What do You Think?

1. Where is commitment strong and weak in your life?

2. How might your relationships and success improve if your commitment were stronger?

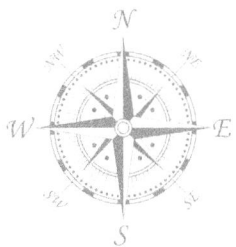

Teamwork:
The Key to Exponential Growth

> *Teamwork: To Collaborate by Doing a Part for the Greater Good*

There has never been a time in history in which teamwork was more important in the business world. Three hundred years ago, nearly all businesses were family-owned and independently run. As cities have grown and technology has increased, so has company size. As the size of our companies and organizations grows, so does our need for teamwork, because the ability of one man or woman to build something on their own simply does not equal the potential of a cohesive whole that works together.

In other words, we can try to keep building our best on our own, but companies that embrace effective teamwork will quickly distinguish themselves from and surpass their more individualistic peers.

There are two obvious components of effective teamwork: the team and the work. This is important for us to understand, because some business-minded leaders simply see the work and as long as the tasks get done, we feel that our business is successful. The truth, however, is that we will enter a much greater realm of success when we recognize that the team accomplishing the tasks is just as significant as the work itself.

Too often, we misalign the tasks and the team so that people are not working within their strengths. Yes, it may be their job to do that particular task, but if a team member has stronger competencies that would enable them to make a greater contribution to your organization, wouldn't it make sense to align them with tasks that draw out their fullest potential? If your company is succeeding when people just do their job, how much more could it thrive if everyone contributed according to their best talents, skills, and abilities?

In many cases, you don't actually need different people in your workforce; you simply need to align the people you have with what they accomplish most naturally. And, it should go without saying, it is still important for tasks to be done and goals to be accomplished. This will happen most productively when people can flourish in doing what they do best, which is not always what they are trained in or hired to do.

How do you strike this delicate balance between building your people and getting things done? You do it by focusing on something that is greater than both team and tasks—**the vision**.

Teamwork holds a bulls-eye to the goal. Everyone aligns around one common purpose and strategically directs their talents, ideas, and solutions toward that goal. When we align around vision and purpose, it doesn't matter who contributed what part. We celebrate the integration of the parts that lead to success and everyone can clearly see their individual significance because they know they contributed something to the whole that only they could contribute.

Focusing on the goal lifts everyone's eyes off of themselves, raising them to the maturity that realizes their own talent, but also their own limitations. **Teamwork strengthens the whole by aligning people with complimenting strengths so that the organization receives the benefit of everyone's best while not being held back by individual limitations.**

This kind of teamwork produces immediate results, but the long-term benefit is even greater. As a culture that celebrates teamwork continues over time in an organization, trust grows and people learn to become even better at the things in which they naturally excel. This increasing trust and competency causes an organization to increase in efficiency and employee engagement and satisfaction, distinguished in its market as a producer of excellence, resilient in times of industry change and transition.

These are distinctions that are simply impossible to attain individually; they are only possible through implementing a culture of teamwork over time. Are you ready to embrace this change and leap into a better future?

Teamwork: Johnsonville Sausage

The Johnsonville Way declares, "We will [become the best company in the world] as each one of us becomes better than anyone else at defining, and then serving, the best interests of all those who have a stake in our success.... As an individual, I understand the Johnsonville Way is about my performance and my accountability to the team."[1]

That's how seriously Johnsonville Sausage takes teamwork. But it wasn't always that way.

The small-town sausage company had grown to about 125 employees by 1982 under the leadership of Ralph C. Stayer, son of the founder. The company was growing, but Stayer could see that it was not healthy. He says of that time, "I made all the decisions. My whole focus was on how I had to change our people." Employee turnover was high and quality suffered.[2]

Stayer hired an expert in company leadership, who told him, "You've got to change you. Don't worry about them, because if you act different, they'll be different." This began a process that gave birth to The Johnsonville Way. [3]

These days, Stayer says, "Other companies use their people to build a business, but at Johnsonville we use our business to build our people."[4] They call their employees, "Members," and their supervisors, "Coaches," in order to shift the primary focus from the job to the team. Current president Bill Morgan puts it this way, "Our philosophy…is together we create an environment where every one of our members is required to develop their God-given talents."[5]

Johnsonville's reinvigorated workforce has now grown to nearly 1,500 employees who support distribution to thirty countries, all for a company that claims number one market share for their industry in the nation.[6]

Embracing teamwork, as it turns out, was Stayer's best business decision.

What do You Think?

1. What is the best team you've been a part of? What made it the best?

2. How can you build those attributes within your current team at work and at home?

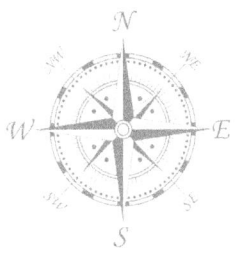

Integrity:
The Inside Truth

> *Integrity: To Have Moral Soundness, Free from the Influence of Corruption*

Everyone knows that integrity is core to building trust, developing relationships, and experiencing fulfillment in life. Why, then, does it feel so unattainable?

It is true that a perfect standard of integrity eludes us, but just as true is that a respectable level of integrity is obtainable. Integrity becomes possible when we start with an important premise—**integrity is not something we can attain by following a set of external rules**. Adjusting our natural behaviors to fit external rules only works for so long before who we really are shows through to the surface.

That is why an organization's values must precede rules and regulations. Not long ago, I facilitated a leadership workshop in Orange County, California, with Clarient Inc. The group enthusiastically embraced conversations about the values driving their organization, but was much less engaged in discussions about setting behavioral expectations. That is counter-intuitive, because many leadership teams focus exclusively on behaviors. As Sherrie Kline, the Senior HR Director, explained, "We were recognized as the best place to work in Orange County because we realize that cultivating integrity is an inside-out process. 'Being' what we value and believe is the true meaning of integrity. Behaviors flow out of who we are and what we value and believe."

Behaviors, rather than being the product of rules, are simply indicators of what lies beneath. This means that the success of both individuals and organizations is proportional to their integrity. Stephen M.R. Covey demonstrates this principle in his book *The Speed of Trust*, showing that integrity (living what we authentically value and believe) establishes trust and is pivotal to individual, team, and organizational success.

Integrity originates in the values and beliefs we hold and is proven when difficult choices arise. If we value people for their inherent worth, we will behave differently than someone who believes people are to be used for personal gain. If we value commitment regardless of the sacrifice, we will behave differently than if we believe that promises can be broken for a better opportunity. If we believe our mission is to benefit the world, we will behave differently than if we believe our mission is to satisfy our own needs.

The following are some steps to identifying the strong and weak aspects of your integrity, working through the principle of reverse engineering to bring you to your desired outcome:

- Identify one specific situation that brought fulfillment or resulted in dissatisfaction and/or disappointment recently.

- Identify one or more specific actions or behaviors you chose in that situation. How well did that work for you? For others?

- What emotions did you experience prior to choosing that behavior?

- What were your primary thoughts about the situation before you acted? What assumptions were made? What alternative perspectives are possible?

- What values and beliefs played into the thoughts you experienced? Did you act out of your core values and beliefs? Did you concede to external pressures, fears, worries, or anxieties?

The secret to building a life of integrity begins with a willingness to look deep within our inner core and determine what we actually value and believe. Once a person has taken this honest assessment, they can build personal goals with strength and durability. The result is integrity, that elusive attribute we all want.

Integrity: Ken Melrose

Ken Melrose took over a failing Toro company in 1983. He knew that turning things around required long-term solutions, so he implemented a culture change. The values he instilled have guided the company to a 700 percent increase in sales—but it hasn't always been easy to hold to those values.[1]

For example, despite Toro's efforts to make safe products, using a lawnmower can cause injury and mis-using it can make that much more likely. This has led to lawsuits against the company. Toro's policy for many years was to fight through litigation, going to court on about half of the lawsuits filed against them. But one day, the product liability team suggested that this practice violated the company's values.

They proposed a solution and Toro implemented their recommendations. It worked so well that now two-thirds of the cases are settled outside of mediation, while one-third go to mediation. Only one case since 1991 has gone to court. The average settlement is over 50 percent less and settled in months rather than years.

What's more, they are able to retain customers who were previously lost.

In another example, Toro's commercial zero-degree mowers had a problem of rolling when used on steep inclines or wet grass. Toro redesigned the product to include roll bars, but this only protected new customers. Even though it meant taking a $25 million hit, the company offered free installation of roll bars to all previous customers, simply because they believed it was the right thing to do.[2]

Ken Melrose and the Toro team pursued consistency between their corporate values and business practices. Integrity didn't come easily or without real cost, but it is the key to the success they enjoy today.

What do You Think?

1. How have your values and beliefs been challenged at work?

2. What behaviors on the outside don't conform to the values and beliefs you hold on the inside?

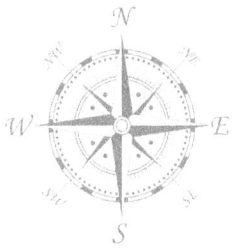

Excellence:
Giving Your Best at All Times

> *Excellence: To Have Distinguished or Superior Quality*

Leaders set the bar. Those following them will rise to whatever example they set. If they work with energy and enthusiasm, it increases the odds that their entire team will do the same. If they demonstrate honesty and integrity in their ethics, the chances increase that their department will follow. For this reason it is important for leaders to demonstrate excellence.

Excellence is an across-the-board attribute. It comes from the heart of a person, affecting everything they do and how they relate to others. As Mario Andretti said, "Desire is the key to motivation, but it's determination and commitment to an unrelenting pursuit of your goal—**a commitment to excellence**—that will enable you to attain the success you seek."[1]

It is very easy to expect excellence from others without truly examining ourselves to make sure that we are setting the example for them to follow. No one will be inspired to follow excellence as a rule, but nearly everyone is inspired by excellence as an example. Steve Jobs reminded us to "Be a yardstick of quality. Some people aren't used to an environment where excellence is expected."[2] **It's good that we expect excellence. It's better that we demonstrate it.**

We can see clearly how excellence affects performance. I remember all the cars my family owned when I was growing up, and it wasn't very many because we drove cars pretty much until they died. But let's just say that it didn't take very long for one of our cars to reach that point. It died very quickly. I remember my mom joking about how it must have been made on a Monday or a Friday because whoever built the car was either looking forward or backward toward their weekend instead of being attentive to their work. She knew that the car was not made with excellence and we were the ones who suffered for it. That experience so colored our view of that brand of cars that every family member has stayed far away from it since.

Excellence also affects relationships. The truth is that there are several elements that work together to build healthy relationships, including things like communication, conflict resolution skills, the ability to establish healthy boundaries, and others, but if we settle for being mediocre at these things then we will only have mediocre relationships at best.

No one wants mediocre performance or relationships, so why do we have less than excellence in these areas? It has to do with integrity and personal accountability. **Integrity provides the inner standard that compels us to excellence even when no one is looking.** But almost everyone has off days, gets tired, or has stressful periods of life that make distraction come more easily. Those are the days when accountability is important.

I know that many people, if not most, have a negative view of accountability because their experience has consisted solely of having someone point out all their mistakes. This may be part of the accountability process, but it should only be a small part. **When accountability is done well, it accounts for your ability.** It measures how high your potential is and then encourages you to rise up to it. This may include some level of processing through failures, but it always encourages lifting our eyes to imagine what is possible.

Also, it's worth noting that healthy accountability comes from trusted leaders or peers in our lives who help us rise to our fullest potential. These people have a responsibility to keep us accountable in the same way that we are responsible for holding our employees accountable. But when we remember what accountability really is and that it ideally comes from people we trust, it becomes a warm blanket instead of a smothering weight.

Excellence even affects community. We're more familiar with negative examples than positive ones—Enron, BP, banks in the housing crisis, government—but all of these arose from a lack of thorough excellence. Imagine the difference if companies maintained excellence across the board and the impact that would have in the lives of the employees as they took that excellence into their homes and neighborhoods. What if those who served on our nation's school boards and city councils could transfer the excellence from our businesses to the other places where they serve?

Consider also the impact that excellence has on our corporate reputation. One brand has notably built its reputation on reliable excellence: Toyota. For years, this one attribute is what set them apart from most other car manufacturers and enabled them to have growing market-share for 30 years in a row. That incredible string of growth ended when the trust they had built with the market was damaged because of the deadly issue of unintended acceleration.[3] This lapse of their tradition of excellence cost as many as 34 lives, numerous injuries, and an unknown amount of vehicle damage that went unreported.[4] These costs are the real issue, but the $3.1 billion Toyota paid out in settlements and the money lost from sales they otherwise would have had is also significant.[5] By all accounts, Toyota has returned to their excellence of old, but this is a sharp price to pay for any temporary compromise.

Excellence is not perfection; it is productive pride to utilize the talents, experience, and abilities we have to give each moment our best effort. We cannot bury our talent, get sloppy with talent, or give anything short of our best, especially as leaders.

Let excellence be our expectation, and let it be our example, for as each part of our organization becomes excellent in what they do best, leveraging their strengths for the good of the whole, our organizations will thrive and we—individually, organizationally, and our communities—will see the impact of excellence.

Excellence: Cheryl Bachelder

The most important mark of leaders who desire excellence is their ability to demonstrate it to such degree that their presence in a company helps those around them to be excellent as well. This is the case for Cheryl Bachelder, CEO of AFC Enterprises, the parent company of Popeyes Louisiana Kitchen.

Bachelder has a track record for excellence throughout her whole life. She graduated college with dual B.S.-M.B.A. degrees at the age of 22. By 32 she was a vice president at Nabisco. Finally, in 2007 she moved to AFC Enterprises, bringing her excellence with her.[6] During her time there, the company's stock has appreciated over 300 percent, showing the market's recognition of growing excellence in the franchising organization.[7]

Just how does Bachelder help to produce such excellence wherever she goes? The Popeyes philosophy is, "How we do business is more important than what we choose to do." Popeyes employees make their relationship with their franchisees their highest priority.[8] When they pursue excellence in serving their franchisees, the franchisees pass that excellence on to their managers, who pass it on to their staff, who present it one piece of chicken at a time to customers.

Bachelder once wrote, "Preparation and practice are gifts that a leader gives to their team....There is no way to get ready to serve the guest well if the team is unprepared when the doors open."[9]

In other words, when leaders demonstrate and teach excellence in their position, it inspires and empowers those around them to perform excellently too. Excellence at Popeyes puts them at the summit of their industry in financial performance—a measure of team, franchise, and customer satisfaction. People buy Popeyes Chicken both because it is excellent and because the franchises operate with excellence, just like CEO Cheryl Bachelder.

What do You Think?

1. How do you demonstrate excellence and help those around you be excellent?

2. Identify a person who has under-used potential. How can you encourage that person to contribute their best?

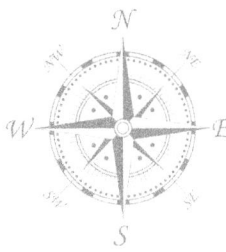

Compassion:
Having Heart in the Workplace

> *Compassion: To Feel and Act Out of Concern for Others*

Leaders are people who get things done. They fix their eyes on a vision and press on until they attain it. But the greatest leaders have another trait that we cannot overlook—we know they care about us.

Yes, we want our leaders to lead and get things done, but we also want to know that they're thinking of us as well. Just to prove that this really is the case, think of someone to whom you have reported who obviously did not think about you and your role when they were making decisions. It probably meant that you ended up needing to work harder and conjure up more energy to stay motivated and engaged.

Compassion in the workplace might sound scary to many of us. Perhaps it brings pictures to mind of an environment filled with emotional expression, affectionate gestures, and a crossover into personal life that hinders productivity. We need to realize that those pictures are an exaggeration of what the reality can and should be.

So what does compassion look like in the work world? I actually experienced a good example of this when I was working my summer job through college. I had worked for the same retail company for several summers in different locations, gaining experience with several managers along the way. But during my last summer working for this company, personal tragedy struck.

I received the bad news after closing hours and called my manager before my scheduled shift the next day. **Without me asking, he offered to give me the day off.** I came in the following day to find that one of my coworkers had bought me a meaningful gift to express her condolences. Another coworker bought me lunch. They were simple tokens of compassion, but it was incredible to see the lasting significant impact that these had as I recovered in those next few months. And, by the way, a lot of work got done that day, completely unhindered by these acts of compassion.

Two things stand out from this experience that help put the power of compassion in perspective. First, the significance came from its wholehearted expression. I had been a strong performer for this company over several years, but I would not have asked for the day off. It meant a lot that **my manager did not wait to be reactively compassionate, choosing instead to be proactive about it.** He offered compassion without any solicitation from me.

Second, my manager's wholehearted example gave permission for other staff members to step up in equally meaningful ways. In this way, it became not just an example, but a culture within our store.

No life is perfect, and everyone in the workplace will go through difficult seasons of life. Compassion simply recognizes this as fact and then proactively develops a culture in which people feel valued and protected when their imperfections show or life takes a bad turn.

We express compassion in the workplace in the everyday things—letting a colleague's sharp words roll off our shoulders when we know they are under stress, or putting a hand on someone's shoulder when we know they are burdened. At one company I worked for, employees could donate sick days and vacation to a family in crisis. Another company I know of chose to extend over-the-top compassion to an employee who was caught stealing through falsified expense reports. They confronted the person, but after much discussion chose not to fire him. The employee received this compassion and became a loyal, honest, and amazing employee.

"Compassion is...the knowledge that there can never really be any peace and joy for me until there is peace and joy finally for you too," said Frederick Buechner.[1] Compassion rises from the ability to imagine ourselves experiencing another person's circumstances and then acting toward them in a way that encourages them, gives them strength, and helps them. The opposite happens when we pass judgment on people, assuming that they are just weak or have a low tolerance level. It can also happen when we are too afraid to involve ourselves in other people's problems. But when we take the step to imagine ourselves in the other person's situation, we quickly realize that **sympathy is meaningless without action.**

Every leader has an opportunity to create a culture where employees feel valued, honored, and supported. In being proactive to an employee's situations and needs, leaders show others that a wholehearted approach isn't weakness.

It's actually the opposite. Compassion has impact and creates strength in the company as individuals are able to draw from within and sympathize with others. One of the greatest outcomes of compassion is that it connects, protects, and uplifts others, creating a bond of cohesion that endures across time.

Clearly, compassion is not weakness. It is the scaffolding that undergirds loyalty, dedication, and commitment.

Compassion: Southwest Airlines

Southwest Airlines was built because the owners valued compassion. When Herb Kelleher and Colleen Barrett surveyed what was the industry at the time, they saw that the only people who could afford to fly were businessmen. They determined to make an airline that allowed the common person to fly. They wanted grandparents to be able to see their grandchildren grow up, and friends to be able to connect during happy or sad times. This was the vision that started their company and it continues to drive the company today.

Importantly, Southwest backs this vision with action. Once, a pilot held the plane at the gate for an extra ten minutes so that a grandfather could travel to see his dying grandson. Despite the fact that on-time service is so important in their industry, Southwest leadership wrote letters to praise him for his actions.[2]

Another time, a ticket counter employee named Rachel was approached on Christmas Eve by an old man with a cane. He quietly asked for a ticket to New

Orleans. Unfortunately there were no more flights that day. He was clearly confused by the situation, but instead of dismissing the man, Rachel discovered that he recently had had heart bypass surgery and had been dropped off at the curb to catch a flight to New Orleans alone. On the busy night, Rachel arranged a wheel chair, escort, hotel, meal tickets, shuttle service, and a cheaper ticket for the first flight the next morning. As they parted ways, both began to cry, one from compassion felt, the other from compassion experienced.[3]

The value of compassion that Southwest holds not only makes it a fulfilling place to work, it also is one of the many reasons Southwest gets rave reviews from its passengers. Southwest demonstrates what it is to have heart in the workplace, and act out of concern for others every day.

What do You Think?

1. What inhibits compassion in your work environment? Homelife? Community?

2. Where have you experienced generous compassion in your career? Homelife? Community? How did it feel?

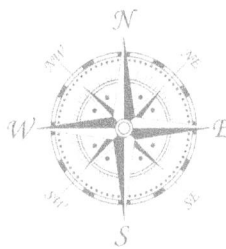

Service:
Leading from Behind

> *Service: To Give of Myself for*
> *Another's Benefit*

There are **two kinds of leadership:** power and service-oriented. Lead by authority, or lead by example.

The world has seen leadership by authority for centuries. We now know that leadership by example is much more powerful and effective. To be on the cutting edge of leadership, we need to embrace service-oriented leadership.

How do the two models differ? Leadership will always maintain its element of authority, but the defining difference is in how that authority is used.

Power leadership sees people as a resource that can be used for any purpose, by any means, for the sake of accomplishing the goals. **Service-oriented leadership** recognizes that the people within our corporations are part of the goals, and thus leads them in such a way that raises them to their full potential. This type of leadership asks employees to fulfill their current job description but it also asks whether there is something even more productive they could be doing, and then assigns them tasks that best utilize their strengths in accomplishing organizational goals.

A power-based leadership structure will always create an **environment of drone workers** who punch the clock, do their job, and go home to their real life. But a service leadership structure will create a **culture of leaders at every level who are engaged** and who actively contribute to the success of the whole.

There are many wonderful examples of service leaders just in the past century or so, including such people as Martin Luther King Jr., John Wooden, John Maxwell, Cathy Truett, and many more. One of the most notable examples, Nelson Mandela, said, "A leader...is like a shepherd. He stays behind the flock, letting the most nimble go out ahead, whereupon the others follow, not realizing that all along they are being directed from behind."[1]

Each of these leaders has stories that validate the power of the service-leadership they lived. But it's especially worthwhile to note that King and Mandela used service leadership to reform oppressive, authoritarian systems. If power leadership was more effective or powerful, then neither King nor Mandela would have succeeded.

We might ask, if service-oriented leadership is so much better, why has it taken so long to be taught? The reason is that it's harder.

In particular, service leadership **requires sacrifice**. It's about putting self aside for the betterment of another person and the overall mission of the organization. The military, top-performing athletic teams, and the most influential leaders of all time deploy this principle. But, truthfully it's easier to be selfish. In fact, it is nearly impossible to yield self-interest in service unless a common cause or mission becomes more important to us than the self-interest we're naturally born with. If we are going to work harder at leadership, we need to understand the benefit we'll receive for the effort.

There is a deeper reason service leadership has been slow to be embraced. After all, entrepreneurs and executives didn't become what they are by taking the easy road. Also, if it just comes down to setting aside our egos, then we really just need to understand the preponderance of evidence proving superiority of the service culture.

Why then would it continue to be difficult to set ego aside? The answer may be that our ego is not really about taking pride in our work or making a difference in our communities. Instead ego thrives on the control we have over other people, and the power we feel from our exalted position.

Taking this one step further, if our identity is rooted in performance-orientation, we risk feeding an ego need to exert authority and make ourselves look good. This approach fears failure above all else and is intimidated by others' successes.

A service-oriented approach is rooted in possibilities and the best interest of others. It bears failure as a steppingstone to success and can celebrate and encourage the successes of others, knowing that the success of one individual provides increased strength to the whole.

What does performance-orientation look like in a real-life work environment? Oftentimes, it simply looks like getting so caught up in our own roles that **we forget the big picture**. For example, a customer service representative within a computer industry may only have the perspective of answering customer questions as fast as possible to meet the "quick response time standard" measure of the department. I've had many customer service reps answer the phone and then disconnect the line. Having come from customer service, I know they are trying to manage down their talk-time numbers. These representatives lose sight of the bigger picture—providing service so that a customer can purchase the right product or service.

Sales people and customer service people are often at odds with each other in companies because the sales people want to book the business (regardless of the policies) and the customer service people adhere to protocols and procedures sometimes without using personal judgment. When something like this example happens, it's easy for self to become the focus instead of service. But **true service is looking out for the benefit of each other and the customer.**

Service: Darwin Smith

Not many people know about Darwin Smith, and that's the point. He began as a simple in-house lawyer for Kimberly-Clark, but the future dramatically changed for both him and the company one day in 1971 when he was chosen to be the next CEO and chairman of the board.

He operated in that role for the next 20 years until retiring 1991, and is known for saying of his position, "I was just trying to become qualified for the job." He more than qualified for it by taking a company that over 20 years had fallen 36 percent behind the general market in stock performance, and transforming it so that it performed 4.1 times greater than the general market.[2] He led the organization in making bold moves to divest its ownership of several paper mills and focus on strengthening the technology of its products. This paid off dramatically in causing Kimberly-Clark brands such as Kleenex and Huggies to gain No. 1 rankings in market share, elevating the company above its rivals Scott Paper and Procter & Gamble.

Despite all his successes, Smith continually passed credit on to the employees, the managers, his predecessors, and the customers. He led the way in developing continuing education and health programs for his employees. He established a culture of service that looks to hire people who want to make a difference in the world, not just for themselves.

Today, two decades after his death, Kimberly-Clark prides itself on serving one billion people worldwide—all because its CEO believed service was the company's No. 1 goal.

What do You Think?

1. When have you experienced service leadership at work, home or in your community?

2. What fears inhibit a culture of service at work? What are the costs?

 # Perseverance:
Don't Give Up!

> *Perseverance: To Persist Toward a Goal*
> *Even in Difficult Times*

When is the last time you wanted to throw in the towel and walk away? Was it today? Or last week? It just happened for me today! It happens to the best of us. But, successful people don't do what they feel. They do whatever it takes to achieve their goal. They persist!

Persistence is the ability to maintain action regardless of how you feel. It means not giving up on the resolve of your heart.

I like James Whitcomb's description of persistence:

> "The determination never to allow your energy
> or enthusiasm to be dampened by the
> discouragement that must inevitably come."[1]

I believe each of us is custom made for a unique purpose in life. Most of us dream big dreams and hope big hopes. Yet, studies show that less than 5% of us actually achieve our dreams and hopes. Why is the success rate so low? It is partly because we lack persistence. We give up when the going gets tough. We question our abilities and the sensibility of the goal. We lose sight of courage as we smack into the mountain of adversity and trial. Our dreams splatter and we fall into the valley of complacency and mediocrity. But, it does not have to be that way!

"In the confrontation between the stream and the rock, the stream always wins, not through strength, but through persistence."[2]

-H Jackson Brown

Let's consider what it takes to be as persistent as a stream:

- **Knowing who we are** – A stream knows its strength lies in the power of repetitive movement. It simply flows in the current of who it is until it sculpts out the path it envisions.

- **Know where I am going** – the stream follows a nature course it was destined to follow. No matter what obstacle it encounters, it flows through, under or over the obstacle to its natural destination.

- **Live in the moment** – the stream encounters each moment sequentially. It doesn't get distracted by the past or the future.

- **Find your passion** – the stream carries energy (passion) that is not easily curtailed by the strength of its opposition. That energy turns problems into solutions.

Let's examine some of the key attributes of Persistence:

- Courageous
- High integrity
- Resiliency
- Intrinsically motivated for a purpose
- Objectivity
- Learner
- Resolved
- Goal oriented

Take a look at some obstacles you may be facing right now. Are you feeling discouraged? Questioning your goals? Just remember that each obstacle that you overcome makes you stronger and more able to power through the next! Focus your mind on the attributes of persistence and the end goal and realize obstacles are only temporary.

In closing I must share one of my favorite quotes on persistence that I often read as my own reminder to stay the course.

"Nothing in the world can take the place of Persistence. Talent will not; nothing is more common than unsuccessful men with talent. Genius will not; unrewarded genius is almost a proverb. Education will not; the world is full of educated derelicts. Persistence and determination alone are omnipotent. The slogan 'Press On' has solved and always will solve the problems of the human race."[3]

-Calvin Coolidge

Perseverance: Katharine Graham

Summit Day
Photo by Charlie Fowler Photography

Katharine Graham never meant to be who she became. Nevertheless, perseverance to grow personally and take challenges head on made her into one of the greatest leaders of the 20th century.

Her father purchased the *Washington Post* in 1933, and Katharine married Philip Graham, who would become its publisher. She lived as a homemaker, as she was raised to do, but when her husband committed suicide in 1963 she essentially inherited his position with the *Post*. It was assumed that she would either sell or hand control over to someone with more experience. However, she retained the position and held it firmly through some of the fiercest trials that not just a business, but America as a nation has ever experienced.[4]

Graham was head of the *Post* when the paper obtained a copy of the Pentagon Papers in 1971. Against her legal department's advice, Graham chose to publish the document, entering a battle with the U.S. government that would only intensify. In 1972, two Post reporters were responsible for breaking open the Watergate scandal. Graham held to her convictions, enduring death threats and presidential pressure to expose governmental corruption.[5]

Graham's self-described most difficult business experience was a 139-day strike by the pressmen's union in 1975 and 1976 that began when workers set fire to one press and severely damaged the others. It ended when replacement workers were hired.[6]

Through all these things, Katharine Graham persevered and rose to become one of the few female heads of a Fortune 500 company—and more than that, she became a history maker.

What do You Think?

1. Identify a dream or hope worthy of persistence.

2. What 1 or 2 strategies will you put in place to stay resolved in persistence?

90

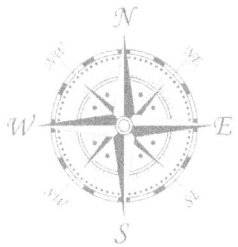

Forgiveness:
Unlocking Bottom-Line Success

> *Forgiveness: To Restore the Standard of Excellence when Character Has Been Violated*

People are different.

I know, that must be the most profound statement you've read all year. But it's an important reality for us to embrace.

Let's start with our background and upbringing. Consider that no two siblings are truly alike, not even identical twins, even though they are raised in the same way by the same parents in the same environment. And, if you've had siblings, you know that siblings still have conflict from time to time. Despite all their natural-born similarities, they can still hurt one another. How much more is this possible among people of diverse background?

Or think about communication styles. Most of us have experienced moments in our lives when, even though everyone in a conversation is speaking English, you could swear that you are not all speaking the same language. This is because there are many complex varieties of communication styles that influence what we mean by what we say, which can create miscommunication and violated expectations, leading to hurt feelings.

So, people are different, yet human nature is to assume that all people are like us. We see the world not the way that it is, but the way that we are. And here you are as a leader tasked with responsibility to manage, lead, cast vision for, and support the diverse group of people under you.

Most people mean well. Almost no one intends to do harm or cause hurt as they interact with other people. Nevertheless, if for no other reason than our differences and normal human assumptions, people still get hurt.

When one employee hurts another, trust is broken—which slows the speed of their interaction, which slows the efficiency of the work they do, which affects the bottom line. Most often, these injuries are relatively minor, but they can accumulate over time until they create employee disengagement and dissatisfaction within the workplace. Soon, the injured employee is looking for another employment position because they don't want to come to a place they perceive as painful. Then of course we need to hire and train someone new.

What if we could stop this process and fix things before we lose our investment? The good news is we can, and the solution is clear.

Whenever this solution is needed, there will be two sides that need to be addressed. First, what is required from the offending party is a change of mind and heart. This alteration needs three things: ownership, apology, and change.

It doesn't make any difference if we've made a big mistake or a small one, we need to take ownership of our mistakes, admit to them, apologize, fix the problem, and then do everything we can not to repeat the problem. As John C. Maxwell once said, "A man must be big enough to admit his mistakes, smart enough to profit from them, and strong enough to correct them."[1]

Second, what is required from the wounded party is forgiveness. "Forgiveness," said Indira Gandhi, "is a virtue of the brave."[2] Courage emerges from the faith in yourself and others to do better.

It is very important for us to realize that forgiveness is not equivalent to trust. You aren't expected to accept or ignore an injustice by forgiving. You simply release the injustice so that it doesn't bog you down in bitterness and resentment. Forgiveness recognizes that punishment and vengeance are not our job, and sets the stage for potential reconciliation.

Reconciliation is always the goal for those who've broken trust. It is that achievement that sets our workplaces in working order again and establishes the foundation upon which we can build more trust for even greater efficiency and productivity.

You now have the key to powerful workplace relationships. No mistake or injustice is beyond forgiveness when people set their hearts and minds to that purpose. If your trust has been broken, you can release yourself of its effect by choosing to forgive and open the door to reconciliation.

In the end, reconciliation always deepens the overall satisfaction, cohesion, and collaboration of people, teams, and organizations. Choose forgiveness!

Forgiveness: Nelson Mandela

Imagine that you were born in a nation governed by people who called you subhuman. During your entire life, you were relegated to whatever leftovers the ruling population didn't want. When you tried to win justice for yourself and the millions of others like you, the government threw you into hard-labor prison for 27 years during which they rarely allowed you to see your family, even forbidding you to attend the funerals of your mother and your son.[3]

Now imagine that at the age of 75, after a lifetime of suffering and a mere 4 years after your release from prison, you have been elected president of this very nation.[4] For the first time in your nation's history, the repressed majority finally has the power and authority to avenge its sufferings—that power and authority rests in your hands.

What would you do?

Nelson Mandela was given this choice. He responded by placing his jailors in the honored front seats at his inauguration, right across the aisle from his family.[5] This symbolic gesture was a powerful example of forgiveness to a country that had seen enough of the damage that anger and bitterness cause. It provided inspiration and true leadership for a diverse nation to enter a new and unified reality.

In a continent that has been tormented by civil war and tribal brutalism, South Africa followed Nelson Mandela on the only path out of that cycle—the path of forgiveness.

What do You Think?

1. What mistakes or injustices do you need to forgive in order to release offense and resentment?

2. Is there any relationship you harmed, even unintentionally, that deserves an apology and reconciliation?

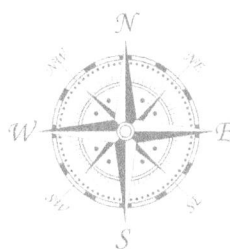

Legacy:
Creating Success that Outlives Us

> *Legacy: To Make a Lasting Contribution in the World*

How do you define success? Building a profitable business and achieving life goals, such as a nice house, good schools for your kids, and a comfortable retirement? These are perfectly normal and respectable marks of success for many people, but there is a higher standard for great leaders.

The ultimate measure of successful leadership has to consider our service and leadership, both of which necessarily involve people outside of ourselves. **If we are the only ones benefited by our success, then we have failed in both service and leadership** because we have served no one but ourselves and, having reached the end, found that no one is truly following us.

This is why, perhaps more than any other measurement, the measure of successful leadership is legacy.

Legacy has an important distinction from most other leadership values in that the other values express the character we have in doing what we do, but legacy expresses why we do what we do. Legacy lifts us out of any focus on what is immediately in front of us and sets our eyes on something bigger, something that impacts those around us in a meaningful way, and something that outlives us.

John Adams once wrote in a letter to his wife, Abigail, "I must study politics and war, that our sons may have liberty to study mathematics and philosophy. Our sons ought to study mathematics and philosophy, geography, natural history and naval architecture, navigation, commerce and agriculture in order to give their children a right to study painting, poetry, music, architecture, statuary, tapestry and porcelain."[1] This vision for legacy was so powerful that it compelled one of America's chief founding fathers to sacrifice whatever it took to produce something so great that not only his children and grandchildren, but hundreds of millions of people throughout the world have now reaped the benefit of it.

That is how powerful legacy can be, but it is actually very simple in practice. When I think of legacy, I think of my childhood coach, Carol Gustofson (we called him Gus). This man invested his whole life in helping kids in north Minneapolis, Minnesota, develop character and hope as he coached them and taught them to swim. When I was about eight years old, he identified me as a strong swimmer and encouraged my parents to put me on the swim team. Through his encouragement and belief in me, I excelled in swimming. But, that wasn't enough for him. He wanted to develop character and leadership in me. At times this was uncomfortable for me. More than once, I cried to my dad because "Gus was picking on me." I see in hindsight that he saw something in me that I would not have seen in myself - and he both taught it into me and encouraged it out of me. His legacy lives on in me today as I do my best to pay that legacy forward.

Legacy is powerful. It burns a passion inside of us that can't be extinguished by circumstances around us. Our drive to accomplish that burning passion spurs us to utilize all of our talents and abilities in service to others. In the end, it is legacy that brings fulfillment and significance to our life. Find your legacy and you find true meaning and purpose.

Legacy: Ken Blanchard

Ken Blanchard's name is so synonymous with leadership that he needs little introduction. He has published more than 30 best-selling books,[2] placing him in rarified company as of 2005 as Amazon's 15th highest best seller.[3] His work has changed the way companies all over the world lead and manage. Yet when he thinks of how he wants to be remembered, he doesn't talk about any of this.

When asked about his legacy, Blanchard said that the epitaph that he enjoys thinking about would say, "All used up." And by that he means that he did what he was supposed to do—love his family, friends, and associates; love what he did; and work to make the world a better place.[4]

In other words, Blanchard wants to be remembered as someone who lived what he taught others to do. He teaches that people are not your most important resource, but instead that your business is people—they are the only reason your business exists.[5]

A powerful example of Blanchard living out this value comes from when the time his house burned down in 2007. He was in Florida at the time and learned of the trouble from his son, Scott, who lived in the same neighborhood. When Scott first called, he and his parents believed that both their houses were gone. In fact, three witnesses, including a police officer, testified that they saw Scott's house on fire.[6]

Blanchard chose in that difficult moment to see his son's trouble before he would consider his own loss. In the end, despite losing their home of 25 years, Blanchard and his wife, Margie, were able to celebrate that Scott's home was untouched, after all.[7]

As they reflected on that event, they realized that it only further entrenched them in their value for legacy. Margie expressed it best, saying, "The things we lost were the things we held on to, but the things we still had access to were the things we gave away."[8]

Ken's legacy continues on in every person that his life has touched. His desire to be "all used up" means that nothing of his value is lost. As leaders, we are all beneficiaries in his pursuit to make the world a better place.

What do You Think?

1. What would you like your epitaph to say?

2. How are you fulfilling that epitaph in your life now? And in the future?

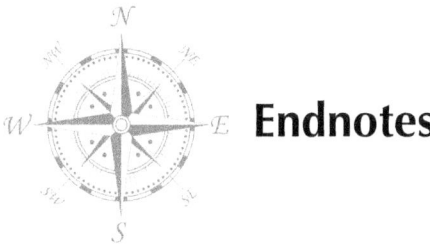

Endnotes

Humility

1 http://www.goodreads.com/quotes/201236-true-humility-is-not-thinking-less-of-yourself-it-is?auto_login_attempted=true

2 http://www.coachwooden.com/index2.html

3 http://www.coachwooden.com/index2.html

4 http://www.coachwooden.com/index2.html

5 Jim Collins. *Good to Great: Why Some Companies Make the Leap...and Others Don't.* New York, New York: HarperBusiness, 2001.

6 Sipe, James W., and Don M. Frick. *Seven Pillars of Servant Leadership.* Mahwah, New Jersey: Paulist Press, 2009. 2.

[7] http://www.washingtonpost.com/wp-dyn/content/article/2010/06/04/AR2010060405169_pf.html

[8] Ibid.

Respect

1 http://www.goodreads.com/quotes/tag/respect?auto_login_attempted=true

[2] http://www.fastcompany.com/3004953/how-sas-became-worlds-best-place-work

[3] http://knowledge.wharton.upenn.edu/article.cfm?articleid=2660

[4] http://www.fastcompany.com/3004953/how-sas-became-worlds-best-place-work

[5] http://knowledge.wharton.upenn.edu/article.cfm?articleid=2660

[6] http://www.fastcompany.com/3004953/how-sas-became-worlds-best-place-work

[7] Ibid.

Honesty

[1] http://www.crunchbase.com/person/andrew-mason

[2] Ibid.

[3] http://www.forbes.com/sites/narrativescience/2013/05/06/forbes-earnings-preview-groupon-3/

[4] http://venturebeat.com/2013/02/28/breaking-andrew-mason-is-out-as-groupons-ceo/#9YFZorRytvvvwliR.99

[5] Ibid.

Trustworthiness

[1] Portrait of Warren Buffett, chairman of Berkshire Hathaway Inc., by Mukul Pandya, from a presentation at a Wharton executive series, April 21, 1999.

Courage

1 http://www.goodreads.com/author/quotes/61105.Dr_Seuss

2 http://www.goodreads.com/quotes/tag/courage?auto_login_attempted=true

Commitment

Photo Credit
Page 45, Commitment: <http://www.123rf.com/photo_3475142_commitment-road-sign-with-dramatic-clouds-and-sky.html>

1 Mandino, Og. *University of Success* New York: Bantam Books, 1982. 44-45.

2 Discovery Press. http://www.discovery-press.com/discovery-press/studyengr/100%20Motivational%20Quotes%20-%20Sports.pdf

3 http://www.quotationspage.com/quote/40271.html

4 http://www.ou.edu/russell/UGcomp/Cascio.pdf

5 ibid

6 http://money.cnn.com/magazines/fortune/fortune_archive/2003/11/24/353755/

Teamwork

1 http://jobs.johnsonville.com/docroot/jobs/pdf/TheJohnsonvilleWay-ThePathWeFollow.pdf

2 http://www.insightonbusiness.com/6240/cover-story-%E2%80%93-fun-on-a-bun-%E2%80%93-johnsonville-president-bill-morgan-leads-the-family-owned-business-as-it-sizzles-on-the-global-scene/

3 Ibid.

4 http://jobs.johnsonville.com/docroot/jobs/pdf/TheJohnsonvilleWay-ThePathWeFollow.pdf

5 http://www.insightonbusiness.com/6240/cover-story-%E2%80%93-fun-on-a-bun-%E2%80%93-johnsonville-president-bill-morgan-leads-the-family-owned-business-as-it-sizzles-on-the-global-scene/

6 http://jobs.johnsonville.com/docroot/jobs/pdf/
TheJohnsonvilleWay-ThePathWeFollow.pdf

Integrity

Photo Credit
Page 58, Supreme Court: <http://www.123rf.com/photo_5576688_
the-front-of-the-us-supreme-court-in-washington-dc.html>

1 http://www.igin.com/article-161-ken_melrose.html

2 http://ethix.org/2007/10/01/caring-about-people-
employees-and-customers

Excellence

1 http://www.brainyquote.com/quotes/quotes/m/
marioandre130613.html

2 http://www.brainyquote.com/quotes/quotes/s/stevejobs126246.
html

3 http://online.wsj.com/article/SB100014241278873246691045782
03440990704994.html

4 http://usnews.rankingsandreviews.com/cars-trucks/daily-
news/100216-Alleged-Death-Toll-Mounts-in-
Toyota-Recall-Cases/

5 http://online.wsj.com/article/SB100014241278873246691045782
03440990704994.html

6 http://www.nytimes.com/2011/01/02/jobs/02boss.html?_r=0

7 http://thepurposeofleadership.com/serving-delivers-superior-
results/

8 ibid

9 http://thepurposeofleadership.com/practice-makes-perfect/

Compassion

1 http://www.brainyquote.com/quotes/quotes/f/frederickb134758.
html

2 http://www.youtube.com/watch?v=yYQV5qK-sH4

3 http://www.customerservicecrossing.com/article/460041/
The-Christmas-Man/

Service

1 http://www.goodreads.com/author/quotes/367338.Nelson_Mandela

2 http://www.paperhall.org/inductees/bios/2004/darwin_smith.php

Perseverance

1 Wilkerson, Carrie. *The Barefoot Executive: The Ultimate Manual for Being Your Own Boss and Achieving Financial Freedom*. Nashville, TN: Thomas Nelson, Inc., 2011. 54.

2 Brown, Jr., H. Jackson. *A Father's Book of Wisdom*. Nashville, TN: Rutledge Hill Press, 1988. 101-05.

3 Morris, Gregory K. *In Pursuit of Leadership: Principles and Practices from the Life of Moses*. Unites States of America: Xulon Press, 2006. 190.

4 http://www.feminine-leadership.com/blog/archives/140

5 http://hbr.org/product/katharine-graham/an/
801276-PDF-ENG

6 ibid

Forgiveness

1 "John Maxwell Quotes," *Sources of Insight*. N.p., 3 Dec. 2011. Web. 17 Sept. 2013. <http://sourcesofinsight.com/john-maxwell-quotes/>

2 Good Quotes, N.p., 2010. Web. 2013. <http://www.goodquotes.com/quote/indira-handhi/forgiveness-is-a-virtue-of-the-brave>

3 http://www.beyondintractability.org/lfg/exemplars/nmandela

4 http://en.wikipedia.org/wiki/Nelson_Mandela#Imprisonment

5 Covey, Stephen. "Lighthouse Principles and Leadership." *UC Morning in America 2.3* (2011): 4.

Legacy

Photo Credit
Page 100, Passing the Baton: <http://www.123rf.com/photo_2973254_hands-passing-the-batton-against-blue-sky.html>

1 http://en.wikiquote.org/wiki/John_Adams

2 http://en.wikipedia.org/wiki/Ken_Blanchard

3 http://www.amazon.com/gp/pdp/profile/A34W7KBHWQ90HC

4 http://www.theleadershiphub.com/videos/ken-blanchard-your-legacy

5 Ibid

6 http://www.kenblanchard.com/news_events/news/?id=1023

7 Ibid

8 http://www.youtube.com/watch?v=6QTFyVrU35w

About the Author

Diane's story begins with her Mid-Western roots. Born and raised in the Twin Cities of Minnesota, Diane grew up believing that values-based character, education, and experiences; strong work ethic; community-focus; and believing in your dreams are core ingredients to living a happy and fulfilled life. While her beliefs and passions have matured and evolved, fundamentally those are the same attributes she believes characterize great leaders of today.

Diane began her career working within Customer Service at American Express Financial Corporation (AEFC) in downtown Minneapolis. She was rapidly promoted into management and became one of the first champions of "self-directed" work teams. AEFC quickly recognized her leadership capabilities, identified her as "High Potential" and supported her completion of a master's degree in Industrial Relations at the University of Minnesota's Carlson School of Management.

At the completion of that program, Diane relocated to San Diego, California, and began her fourteen year career with the highly-esteemed global pharmaceutical company Eli Lilly and Company, which later divested the medical device divisions and became Guidant Corporation. Throughout her tenure, Diane served in a variety of strategic human resource leadership roles, including talent management, technical and professional training, and executive development. Diane led the launch of Guidant's first Work/Life program, which later grew into a strategic Diversity and Inclusion department. For Diane, three key notable factors highlight her Eli Lilly/Guidant experience: development of meaningful relationships, rich leadership experiences, and the opportunity to impact the quality of patients' lives.

In July 2005, Diane launched the Talent Journey. She had no desire to leave the corporate life and relationships she had developed, but felt compelled to extend her reach into diverse types of organizations. Talent Journey's mission was to lead individuals, teams, and organizations to achieve their organizational mission by selecting, engaging, aligning, and developing their collective potential.

In January 2013, Diane renamed her company Blueprint LEADERSHIP. Blueprint leadership is simply leading in such a way as to influence people to take action for the benefit of others. Partnered with a variety of biotech, healthcare, and medical device companies, as well as manufacturing/operations, retail, and educational institutions, Diane teaches, guides, and coaches leaders in building the inside-out transformational Blueprint LEADERSHIP Skills.

www.ingramcontent.com/pod-product-compliance
Lightning Source LLC
Chambersburg PA
CBHW051333170526
45166CB00002B/792